HAL•LEONARD INSTRUMENTAL PLAY-ALONG

AUDIO ACCESS INCLUDED

PLAYBACK+
Speed • Pitch • Balance • Loop

VIOLIN

CHRISTMAS Favorites

Audio arrangements by Peter Deneff

To access audio visit:
www.halleonard.com/mylibrary

Enter Code
8522-7936-6469-6189

ISBN 978-1-4950-9640-2

HAL•LEONARD®

7777 W. BLUEMOUND RD. P.O. BOX 13819 MILWAUKEE, WI 53213

In Australia Contact:
Hal Leonard Australia Pty. Ltd.
4 Lentara Court
Cheltenham, Victoria, 3192 Australia
Email: ausadmin@halleonard.com.au

Visit Hal Leonard Online at
www.halleonard.com

BLUE CHRISTMAS

VIOLIN

Words and Music by BILLY HAYES
and JAY JOHNSON

THE CHRISTMAS SONG
(Chestnuts Roasting on an Open Fire)

VIOLIN

Music and Lyric by MEL TORMÉ
and ROBERT WELLS

CHRISTMAS TIME IS HERE

from A CHARLIE BROWN CHRISTMAS

VIOLIN

Words by LEE MENDELSON
Music by VINCE GUARALDI

FELIZ NAVIDAD

VIOLIN

Music and Lyrics by
JOSÉ FELICIANO

HAPPY XMAS
(War Is Over)

VIOLIN

Written by JOHN LENNON
and YOKO ONO

HAVE YOURSELF A MERRY LITTLE CHRISTMAS

from MEET ME IN ST. LOUIS

VIOLIN

Words and Music by HUGH MARTIN
and RALPH BLANE

HERE COMES SANTA CLAUS
(Right Down Santa Claus Lane)

VIOLIN

Words and Music by GENE AUTRY
and OAKLEY HALDEMAN

(There's No Place Like)
HOME FOR THE HOLIDAYS

VIOLIN

Words and Music by AL STILLMAN
and ROBERT ALLEN

IT'S BEGINNING TO LOOK LIKE CHRISTMAS

Violin

By MEREDITH WILLSON

MELE KALIKIMAKA

VIOLIN

Words and Music by
R. ALEX ANDERSON

MERRY CHRISTMAS, DARLING

VIOLIN

Words and Music by RICHARD CARPENTER
and FRANK POOLER

ROCKIN' AROUND THE CHRISTMAS TREE

VIOLIN

Music and Lyrics by
JOHNNY MARKS

RUDOLPH THE RED-NOSED REINDEER

VIOLIN

Music and Lyrics by
JOHNNY MARKS

SILVER AND GOLD

VIOLIN

Music and Lyrics by
JOHNNY MARKS